SPOTLIGHT ON EXPLORERS AND COLONIZATION™

AMERIGO VESPUCCI

Explorer of South America and the West Indies

HEATHER MOORE NIVER

ROSEN
PUBLISHING®
New York

Published in 2017 by The Rosen Publishing Group, Inc.
29 East 21st Street, New York, NY 10010

First Edition

Library of Congress Cataloging-in-Publication Data

Names: Niver, Heather Moore, author.
Title: Amerigo Vespucci: explorer of South America and the West Indies / Heather Moore Niver.
Description: First edition. | New York : Rosen Publishing, 2017. | Series: Spotlight on explorers and colonization | Includes bibliographical references and index. |
Audience: Grade 7 to 12.
Identifiers: LCCN 2015050279 | ISBN 9781477787953 (library bound) | ISBN 9781477787922 (pbk.) | ISBN 9781477787939 (6-pack)
Subjects: LCSH: Vespucci, Amerigo, 1451-1512. | Explorers—America—Biography. | Explorers—Spain—Biography. | Explorers—Portugal—Biography. | America—Discovery and exploration—Spanish. | America—Discovery and exploration—Portuguese.
Classification: LCC E125.V5 N58 2016 | DDC 910.92—dc23
LC record available at http://lccn.loc.gov/2015050279

Manufactured in the United States of America

CONTENTS

WHO IN THE WORLD IS AMERIGO VESPUCCI?

Two entire contents are named after the explorer, merchant, and navigator known as Amerigo Vespucci. Yet much of his life remains not only a mystery but also a controversy. Curiously, he was hardly known before North America and South America were named after him. He wasn't even the first person to discover what we now know as the Americas. His own voyages occurred several years after Christopher Columbus's infamous first trip.

But Vespucci made major contributions to navigation. For example, he was the first to realize that North and South America were not part of Asia, but entirely separate continents—even Christopher Columbus didn't know that! He also developed a process for measuring longitude.

Various letters with conflicting details and dates makes tracing the history of Amerigo Vespucci a challenge at best. Did he take two trips or four? Some claim he took two more, bringing his lifelong voyages to a grand total of six.

BEFORE THE FAME: AMBASSADOR AND PICKLE SALESMAN

Young Amerigo Vespucci, spelled Americus Vespucius in Latin, is thought to have been born in Florence, Italy, in 1451. However, no one is exactly sure. Some historians think it is more likely that he was born in 1454. He was the youngest of three sons to his parents, Ser Nastagio and Lisabetta Mini. His father, Nastagio, was a notary. As Amerigo grew up, his religious uncle Giorgio Antonio Vespucci educated him, although his brothers studied at the University of Pisa in Tuscany, Italy. From an early age, Vespucci was interested in reading books and maps.

Vespucci's family was close with the famous Medicis, who had been powerful in Italy for three hundred years. His uncle sent him off on one of his first jobs for the Medici family in Cadiz, Spain. Here Vespucci met and became a trusted friend to Lorenzo di Pierfrancesco de' Medici. Vespucci was in charge of the estate of a recently deceased Italian merchant named Giannotto Berardi. He made sure Berardi's contract was taken care of by delivering twelve ships to the crown to sail to the West Indies. Once this contract was fulfilled, Vespucci continued working to supply ships with the supplies they needed.

This illustration of the ship *Great Harry* is similar to the sorts of ships that Vespucci may have stocked in 1499.

Before he set off to sail across the open seas to become an explorer, Vespucci had a number of different jobs. When he was in his twenties, another uncle, Guido Antonio Vespucci, was ambassador of Florence under King Louis XI of France. A job with his uncle sent Vespucci to Paris. Perhaps this trip sparked his interest in travel and exploring.

Other jobs he had before exploring included some in the business trade, which he did only under pressure from his father. According to writer Ralph Waldo Emerson, Vespucci spent some time selling jewels and even pickles! In 1499, he moved to Seville, where he helped stock ships with food, such as preserved meats and other foods.

CONNECTIONS TO CHRISTOPHER COLUMBUS

Vespucci's Medici connection may have helped him get a job working for the family as a banker. Later, he worked as a supervisor for the outfitting of their ships in Seville, Spain. This work, too, may have piqued his interest in exploring the seas.

In 1492, Vespucci officially moved to Spain, where he met explorers and learned about the business of exploring, including how to prepare ships for long voyages.

In 1496, Vespucci worked on the ship of Christopher Columbus. He may have supplied beef for voyages at least twice in his lifetime. Columbus's stories about his

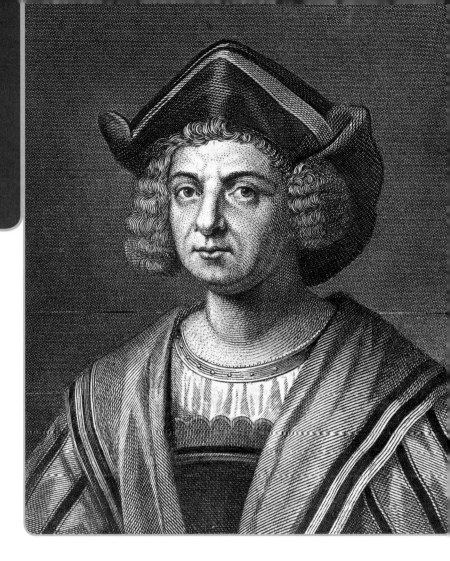

Vespucci may have supplied Columbus's ships with food for their voyages, work that may have inspired Vespucci to set sail himself.

recent trip to America made Vespucci eager to see the New World. By now, Vespucci was in his forties, and his business wasn't thriving in the way he'd hoped. He heard that Spain's monarchs, King Ferdinand and Queen Isabella, might be willing to fund voyages by other explorers.

It was time for Vespucci to set sail.

THE QUESTION OF THE LETTERS

Here, Vespucci's life gets a little murky. It seems that there are two sets of letters that he may or may not have written about his explorations. A first set of two letters claim that he made a total of four voyages. The letters were written in his name, but there is some question as to whether or not he actually wrote them. These two letters were allegedly written on September 4, 1504, and suggest that he made four voyages. They were written in Italian from Lisbon, Portugal, and printed in Florence in 1505. It appears that they were addressed to a gonfalonier, the judge of a medieval Italian state, named Piero Soderini. Two Latin versions of this letter were printed under different titles.

This illustration is from the supposed letters of Vespucci. The story of his expeditions gets confused by the publication of letters later thought to be forged.

Until fairly recently, around 1930, these letters were considered authentic. By some theories, however, these letters were merely masterful misrepresentations and are not to be trusted.

Meanwhile, a second group containing three letters discusses only two voyages.

These letters are addressed to Lorenzo di Pierfrancesco de' Medici, who was both Vespucci's friend and benefactor. Some historians consider these letters to be more personal and more accurate.

These conflicting stories have resulted in historical uproar. Some feel that Vespucci, who enjoyed writing, penned the first group of letters, but that he deliberately fabricated the additional voyages and left out the contributions of others who traveled with him. In the first group of letters, Vespucci is clearly the hero of the story. Many of the dates for the voyages are also incorrect.

Which set of letters is to be believed? Some attempts have been made to work out how the various letters could complement one another, but so far, none of these efforts have been successful.

Still, it's worthwhile to take a look at the voyages, both actual and possibly fictionalized, and examine where Vespucci explored.

Letters Vespucci wrote to Lorenzo de' Medici are thought to be authentic representations of his adventures, although he may have exaggerated a bit.

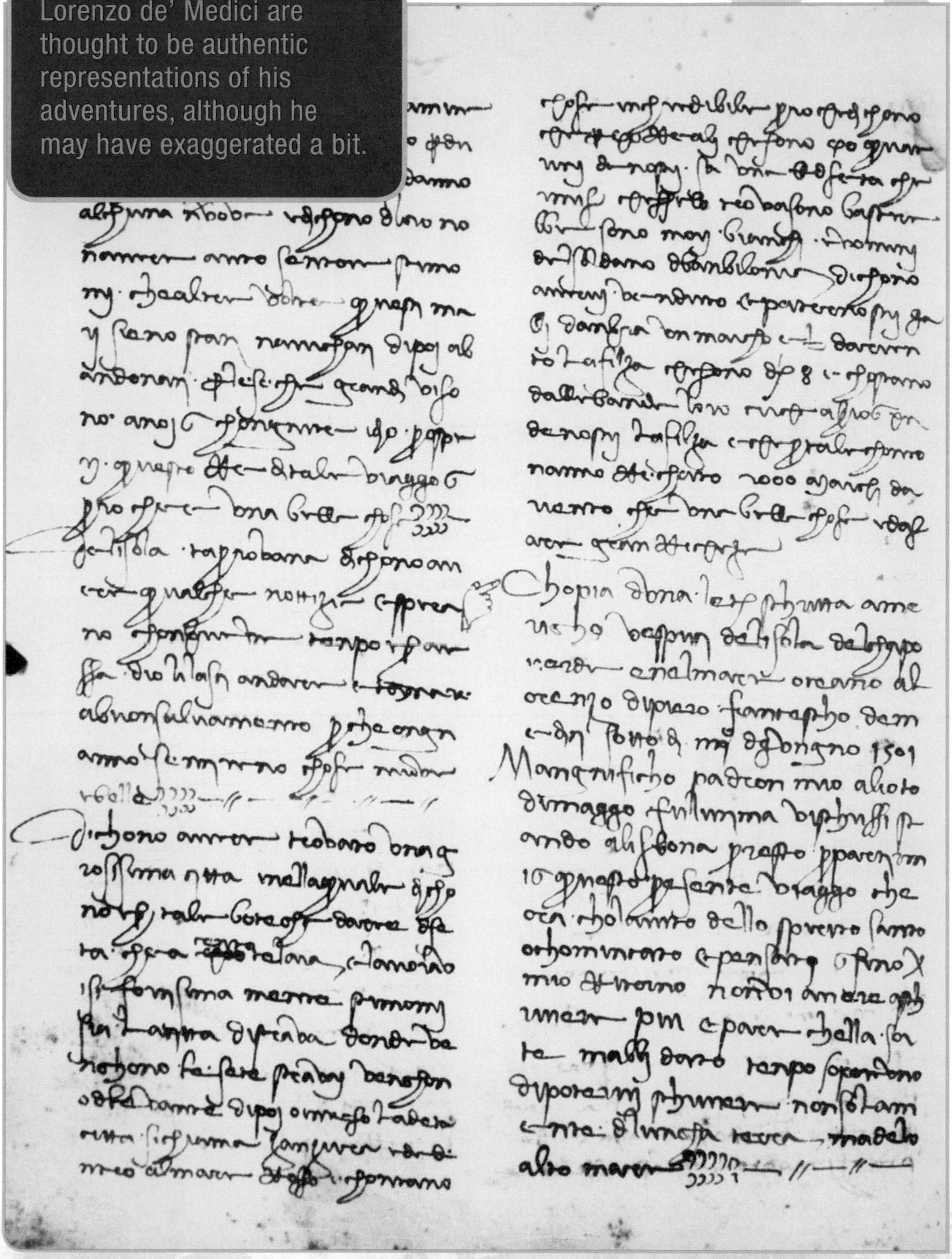

MAIDEN VOYAGE?

According to Vespucci's 1504 letter, the first of his alleged four voyages occurred from 1497 to 1498. He supposedly set sail from Cadiz, Spain, on May 10. With a fleet of ships from Spain, Vespucci spent five weeks sailing through the West Indies, including exploring "the finest harbor in the world," before landing on North America's mainland. Some read his letters to suggest he may have traveled as far north as what we now know as Canada's British Columbia. If this letter were indeed true, it would mean that Amerigo Vespucci had discovered the mainland a full year before Christopher Columbus! By October

1498 Vespucci and the fleet had returned safely back to Spain.

Many scholars don't give this alleged voyage any credit. Perhaps his letters mixed up dates and descriptions, but some suggest Vespucci was deliberately misleading. In any case, records from Spain do not support his claims at all.

This undated illustration of Jamaica in the West Indies depicts the area where the first of Vespucci's alleged four voyages took him before he landed in North America.

1499–1500 VOYAGE

Vespucci's actual maiden voyage more likely occurred in 1499. Christopher Columbus had insisted that he had discovered India, but the Spanish were unsure. Where were the castles of gold and markets teeming with spices they had heard about? Frustrated with Columbus, King Ferdinand and Queen Isabella decided to give other explorers a chance. In 1499, they approved an expedition by Alonso de Ojeda.

Historians aren't certain what Vespucci did on this trip. His name is not included on the crew's records, and some feel that this omission suggests that he just came along as a civilian. Another theory is that the voyage's supporters sent him along to keep

ARRIVAL OF OJEDA AND HIS FOLLOWERS AT THE INDIAN VILLAGE.

Vespucci's first voyage probably occurred on an expedition headed by Alonzo de Ojeda, illustrated here with natives. The role of Vespucci on these voyages is unclear.

an eye on the work that was being done— Vespucci could ensure that their investment in the trip would not go to waste.

Apparently, when they reached what is now the country of Guyana, Vespucci and Ojeda split up. Vespucci's crew headed south to the outlet of the Amazon River.

From there they likely traveled to the Cape of Saint Augustine, in modern-day Brazil. On the return trip, Vespucci recorded having reached Trinidad, the Orinoco River outlet (in present-day Venezuela), and Haiti. He thought that he'd reached a southern peninsula of Asia, so he looked for the tip, which he named Cape Cattigara.

When he returned home, Vespucci wrote one of the authentic letters to Lorenzo di Pierfrancesco de' Medici. Many explorers were infamous for sailing solely in search of riches, but Vespucci's letters were brimming with scientific and anthropological observations. He detailed the native people he'd met when he was in the northern areas of South

America. Some historians note that Vespucci, having sold jewels in his previous business dealings, may have taken this trip to head to Venezuela to procure pearls.

When they reached modern-day Guyana, Vespucci split with Ojeda. His letters detail meeting up with the natives.

DEBUNKING DEAD RECKONING

Several of Vespucci's discoveries on this trip were very important. Of particular importance in his letter to Lorenzo di Pierfrancesco de' Medici is his discovery of a more efficient way to measure longitude. Previously—for centuries, actually—sailors had used a calculation called dead reckoning. They calculated their longitude by guessing where they were in the world based upon where they had been before and how far they had journeyed. Vespucci, however, used celestial observations. Later, John Harrison would invent the marine

chronometer, which allowed sailors to calculate their longitude at sea far more accurately.

Vespucci also made a signficiant contribution to the field of geography by calculating the size of the Earth. He was so specific that he figured out the circumference of the equator to within about 50 miles (80 kilometers) of its actual size. Not bad for a guy who didn't have the modern technology we depend on today!

1501–1502 VOYAGE

Almost as soon as his feet touched solid ground in Spain, Vespucci made plans for another voyage. His aim this time was to sail to the Indian Ocean, the Gulf of the Ganges (known today as the Bay of Bengal), and the island of Taprobane or Ceylon (modern-day Sri Lanka). Unfortunately, the government of Spain was far less enthused by his plan and rejected it.

Instead, he somehow put forth his plans to Portugal, this time for another trip to Brazil, and they were accepted. No one is sure how he managed to convince Portugal's powerful King Manuel I, although it's likely that the king desired the rights to settle there in the future. Nor is it clear why

EMANVEL I. LVSITANIÆ REX XIV.

Emanuel Ferdinando Alphonsi V. fratre natus Ioanni absque liberis defuncto iure sanguinis in Regno succedit aeta-
tis annum tum agebat 26, ut qui ann. 1469. editus fuerat Regnum à Clementia auspicatus, permultos ex Brigantina
familia regii sanguinis exules reuocauit. Sub Emanuele Lusitani eam famam sunt adepti, ut cum Græcis, ac Romani
conferri possint. Cum Vasco Gamma Duce in Orientem alacriter uela dedissent, Superato Bonæ Spei Promontorio, per diffi-
cili sane nauigatione Calecutum, Malabarici Regni Caput, peruenerunt Goa deinde in potestatem redactas, sedes in ea
maximi in Oriente Imperii Emanueli est constituta. Huic paulo post adiecta in sinu Persico Armusia, ac Malacca in Insula quæ ueteribus Aurea Chersonesus fuisse dicitur. In Occidentem uerò Aluarus Capralis ui tempestatis dela-
tus Brasiliam detexit, Ferdinandus Magelianus emenso freto, quod ex illius nomine deinceps est appellatum, Moluccas per-
uasit. Ex Africanis etiam rebus haud minor Emanueli gloria. Neque enim solum oppugnando, sed etiam resistendo plures
eodem tempore earum gentium Reges sæpe clade, atque ignominia affecit. Plura in Lusitania templa, atque ædificia publica excita-
uit quæ pietatis, ac uictoriarum suarum monumenta essent. Ex Maria Castellana Vxore Ioanem Regni hæredem, multosque præterea
utriusque sexus liberos suscepit, fato functus est ann. 1521. annos uixit 52. regnauit 26.

Vespucci wanted to head back to Brazil. Perhaps he was simply curious to explore it some more.

On May 13, 1501, Vespucci set sail from Lisbon, Portugal, and pointed the bow of his ship southwest until he reached Brazil's coast and the Cape of Saint Augustine.

DANTHES Aligerius Florentinus Poëta, Anno Sal. M.CCC. descripsit IIII. ſtellas Antarcticas cap. pr.° purg.

His verbis ab Americo Vespuccio in ſuis Epiſtolis adductis.

Io mi volſi a man deſtra, e poſimente
A l'altro polo, e vidi quattro ſtelle
Non viſte mai fuer ch'a la prima gente,
Goder pareua il ciel di lor fiammelle;
O Settentrional vedruo ſito,
Poi che priuato ſei di mirar quelle.

Ego inde versus intuebar æthera,
Poli Nothi adnotaui ibi aſtra quattuor,
Nisi à priore gente, visa nemini.
Nitet, micatꝗ flamma quadrupla æthere,
Mihi plaga orbis orba noſſe cerneris
Nequit videre quando tanta lumina.

Ioan. Stradanus inuent.   Ioan. Collaert ſculp.

Americ Vespuce observe la constellation de « la Croix du Sud »
D'après un dessin de J. Stradanus gravé par J. Collaert en 1522

Vespucci is illustrated here gazing at the Southern Cross, a constellation usually visible only in the Southern Hemisphere.

Many of Vespucci's claims about this trip are up for debate. According to him, they sailed still further south to Río de la

Plata. If this is true, Vespucci was the first European to enter that estuary. He claims to have sailed on along Patagonia's coast (today part of southern Argentina). There are no records of his return trip's route, but he did return to Lisbon on July 22, 1502.

Vespucci's records show that he closely watched the stars at night. The constellations in the Southern Hemisphere were not the same as those over Europe. He also made more notes about the natives he encountered. Some say it's important to note that he never regarded them as "savages" but simply observed their customs as another way of life.

On his return, Vespucci made a shocking statement, which was published all over Europe: The lands to the west were not Asia, as Columbus had claimed. This was the New World. (Yet again, some historians doubt whether or not Vespucci was the first to coin this term.)

1503 VOYAGE

Another voyage that Vespucci claimed to his name occurred in 1503. If indeed he went, this voyage was for Portugal. His ships were headed for the Strait of Malacca, which is important because it connects the Indian Ocean to the South China Sea. Six ships allegedly departed from Lisbon on May 10, 1503, although some records say they left in June. They were headed at first for Brazil. Another explorer named Gonzalo Coelho may have joined him on this trip.

Alas, not much was discovered, so the fleet was set to break up. But before they set sail, Vespucci realized that Coelho was missing! Apparently, Vespucci sailed onward without finding him. He discovered Bahia, on the eastern coast of Brazil, as

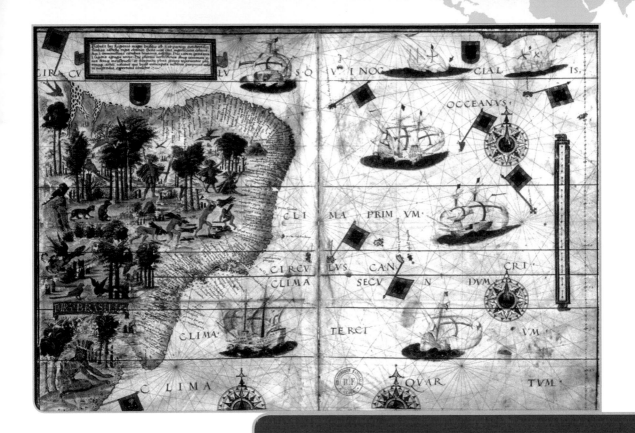

This map of Brazil was likely created by later Portuguese explorers around 1525. Vespucci had discovered Bahia and the island of South Georgia, and he may have built a fort on Cape Frio.

well as an island called South Georgia. Vespucci may have built a fort on Cape Frio, which is right on the Tropic of Capricorn. Here they located a lot of brazilwood, the tree that later gave the nation of Brazil its name.

He returned to Lisbon on June 18, 1504.

WHERE IN THE WORLD WAS VESPUCCI?

The year 1505 was busy for Vespucci, even for an explorer. In spite of debunking Christopher Columbus's claim to have discovered the New World, Vespucci was still friendly with him. In fact, he may have actually lived with the Columbus family in 1505.

Vespucci was naturalized as a citizen of Spain that year. This was made possible by a special royal decree, which later gave him an official title: *piloto mayor de España*. Also this year, Vespucci said wedding vows. He married Maria Cerezo. The two never had any children.

Some historians say that Vespucci never went on another voyage after his trip for Portugal in 1503 and 1504, but others feel he had two more adventures after that, one in 1505, and another in 1507. His 1505 voyage, which would have been his fifth, was allegedly with Juan de la Cosa.

In 1506 Martín Alonso Pinzón had his expedition outfitted by Vespucci. He was not, as some historians say, on his own expedition.

MARTIN A PINZON

They are said to have sailed between May and December that year, visiting the Gulf of Darien in the Caribbean Sea, as well as exploring 200 miles (322 km) into the Atrato River in northwestern Colombia. If this trip in fact occurred, they might have returned with quite a bit of wealth. They are said to have returned with gold and pearls.

It should be noted that neither of these voyages appears anywhere in Vespucci's accounts. On the contrary, his own records show that he was in Spain in 1506, hard at work outfitting an expedition for another navigator named Martín Alonso Pinzón, who had joined Christopher Columbus on his first New World voyage. It appears that Pinzón's voyage never set sail.

Because the details and facts about these two supposed voyages are not confirmed, however, most feel that 1504 was the last time Vespucci sailed the seas on an expedition.

VESPUCCI ON THE MAP!

In 1507 in northern France's Saint-Dié-des-Vosges, some scholars were busy creating a book about geography called *Cosmographiae introduction (Introduction to Cosmography)*. Using this book, readers were able to create their own globes. One of these authors was a German mapmaker named Martin Waldseemüller. He published a booklet of his own entitled "Quattuor Americi navigationes" ("Four Voyages of Amerigo").

In this publication, he suggested renaming the New World: "ab Americo Inventore…quasi Americi terram sive Americam" ("from Amerigo the discoverer… as if it were the land of Americus or

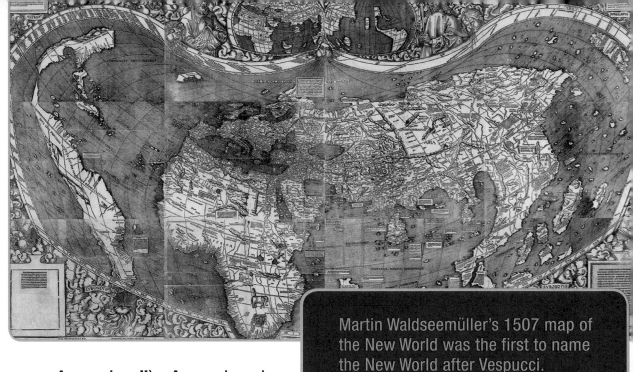

Martin Waldseemüller's 1507 map of the New World was the first to name the New World after Vespucci.

America"). America is the feminine version of Amerigo. This is the first time the name America appears, although Waldseemüller uses it to refer only to South America. Later, it also came to refer to North America. The maps sold like mad, and the name caught on. Vespucci's image appears on the map near the New World. Next to the Old World appears an image of Ptolemy, an astronomer and geographer from the second century CE in Greece.

Waldseemüller is said to have had second thoughts about choosing Vespucci as the namesake of the New World continents.

In fact, on his 1513 version of the map, he decided that Christopher Columbus deserved the honor for discovering the New

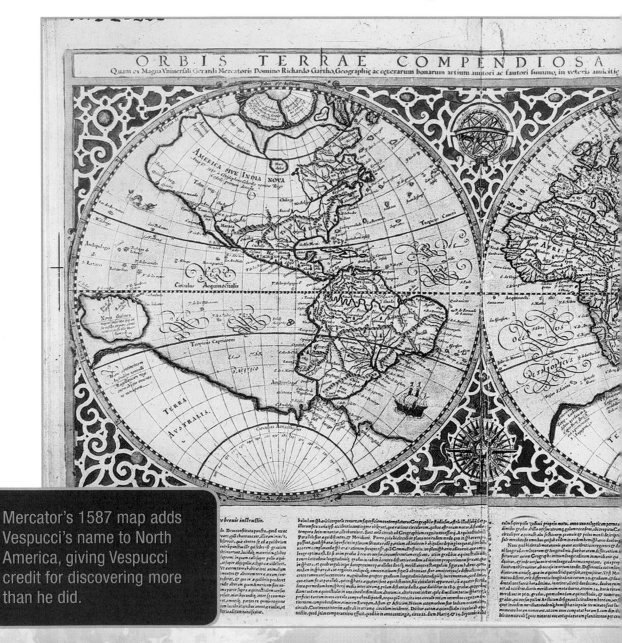

ORBIS TERRAE COMPENDIOSA

Quam ex Magna Vniuersali Gerardi Mercatoris Domino Richardo Gartho, Geographiæ ac cæterarum bonarum artium amatori ac fautori summo, in veteris amicitie

Mercator's 1587 map adds Vespucci's name to North America, giving Vespucci credit for discovering more than he did.

World. Waldseemüller went as far as removing Vespucci's name from the map entirely. He suggested names like Atlantis and Columbiana, but by this time, it was too late! The name had caught on already, and none of the suggested alternatives would ever take its place.

It wasn't until 1538 that North America was named. A mapmaker named Gerardus Mercator referred to the Waldseemüller maps created at Saint-Dié-des-Vosges. In his new maps, he also named the northern part of the content, not just the southern. This resulted in giving Vespucci credit for discovering more territory than he actually did, including areas most historians feel were rightfully credited to Christopher Columbus.

LAST DAYS

During his later life, Vespucci continued to work for Casa de Contratación de las Indias (Commercial House for the Indies). In 1508, he was given a great deal of responsibility when he was appointed as chief navigator. He was charged with closely reviewing each license for every pilot and shipmaster before they were allowed to head out on another voyage. Another part of this job was to create an official map of any recently discovered lands as well as the routes taken to get there. This was all done as a part of a royal survey. Captains were required to give Vespucci all the data they collected on their trips, and he was responsible for deciphering and organizing all this information.

Vespucci worked in this position until he died on February 22, 1512, in Seville, Spain. After his death, his widow, Maria Cerezo, received a pension (money to live on) in honor of her husband's service to the crown.

LEGACY

Amerigo Vespucci's life and legacy continue to puzzle even top historians. Some praise his two more verified explorations and contributions to navigation. Others doubt his words because several letters, after much study and debate, appear to show that he forged at least some of his travels, deeds, and explorations, all perhaps just to bring attention and glory to himself. Still others think that he did not exploit these claims himself, but that others made him out to be more important than he really was. He appears in no way responsible for the inclusion of his likeness or the name America on the Waldseemüller maps.

Regardless, there's no doubt that his travels offered much to history and helped

There are plenty of perplexing accounts of Vespucci's life, but among those that are verified, he did discover the Amazon River.

broaden future explorers' understanding of the larger world. He did discover the Amazon River and, to everyone's surprise, realized that the continent they were exploring was not Asia. His contributions to navigation also allowed sailors to calculate their longitude more accurately.

GLOSSARY

anthropological Referring to the study of humans and their civilizations, cultures, and developments.

benefactor Someone who supports others or a cause with help such as money.

brazilwood A South American tree that produces nuts and can be used for dye

chronometer A marine tool used to keep track of time.

debunk To reveal an idea, myth, or belief to be false.

decipher To decode a mysterious code into everyday language.

decree An authorized instruction given by a legal body.

estuary The part of a river where the freshwater current meets the ocean.

exploit To use something for one's own advantage.

forge To make a copy of something with the intent to deceive.

longitude Degrees of distance measured east to west.

merchant A person who buys and sells or trades items.

naturalized Describing someone, usually a foreigner, who has become a citizen of a certain state or nation.

notary Someone with legal authority, such as to act as an official witness or to draw up contracts.

strait A narrow stretch of water that connects two larger bodies of water.

survey To observe and document an area and its features, such as to create or construct a map.

The Explorers Club
46 East 70th Street
New York, NY 10021
(212) 628-8383
Website: https://explorers.org
Founded in 1904, this organization seeks to uphold
scientific exploration of all mediums by endorsing
study and instruction in physical, natural, and
biological sciences.

The Gilder Lehrman Institute of American History
49 West 45th Street, 6th Floor
New York, NY 10036
(646) 366-9666
Website: https://www.gilderlehrman.org/history-by-
era/exploration/timeline-terms/amerigo-vespucci
The Gilder Lehrman Institute of American History is
a nonprofit organization dedicated to improving
history education through programs for teachers
and students.

Institute and Museum of the History of Science
Piazza dei Giudici 1
50122 Florence
Italy
Website: http://www.museogalileo.it/en/
explore/exhibitions/virtualexhibitions/
amerigovespucciatthemuseum.html
Founded in 1927, the Institute and Museum of
the History of Science is focused on research,

certification, and sharing the history of science. The museum features a library, archives, multimedia, and photographic and restoration laboratories.

The Mariners' Museum
100 Museum Drive
Newport News, VA 23606
(757) 596-2222
Website: http://www.marinersmuseum.org
The Mariners' Museum uses art and relics to teach people about the importance of the sea in the advancement of humankind. It also promotes a recognition of "the maritime world—past, present and future."

Websites

Because of the changing nature of Internet links, Rosen Publishing has developed an online list of websites related to the subject of this book. This site is updated regularly. Please use this link to access this list:

http://www.rosenlinks.com/SEC/ameri

Anderson, Marilyn. *Biographies of the New World.* New York, NY: Britannica Educational Publishing, 2013.

Cooke, Tim. *The Exploration of South America.* New York, NY: Gareth Stevens, 2013.

Curley, Robert. *Explorers of the Renaissance.* New York, NY: Britannica Educational Publishing, 2013.

Fraser, Ian D. *Amerigo Vespucci for Kids!: The Amazing Explorer Who Discovered the Truth About the New World.* Amazon Digital Services, 2015.

Kling, Andrew A. *The Age of Exploration (World History Series).* Detroit, MI: Lucent Books, 2013.

Krull, Kathleen. *Lives of the Explorers: Discoveries, Disasters (and What the Neighbors Thought).* Boston, MA: Houghton Mifflin Harcourt Publishing, 2014.

Lambert, Lorene, and Jed Mickle. *Who in the World Was the Forgotten Explorer?: The Story of Amerigo Vespucci.* Charles City, VA: Peace Hill Press, 2005.

Pletcher, Kenneth, ed. *The Age of Exploration: From Christopher Columbus to Ferdinand Magellan (The Britannica Guide to Explorers and Adventurers).* New York, NY: Britannica Educational Publishing, 2013.

Rajczak, Kristen. *Latitude and Longitude (Map Basics).* New York, NY: Gareth Stevens Publishing, 2014.

Ross, Stewart. *Into the Unknown: How Great Explorers Found Their Way by Land, Sea, and Air.* Somerville, MA: Candlewick Press, 2014.

BIBLIOGRAPHY

Bio. "Amerigo Vespucci Biography." 2015 (http://www.biography.com/people/amerigo-vespucci-9517978#voyages).

Cavendish, Richard. "The Birth of Amerigo Vespucci." *History Today*, March 3, 2004 (http://www.historytoday.com/richard-cavendish/birth-amerigo-vespucci).

History.com. "Amerigo Vespucci." 2015 (http://www.history.com/topics/exploration/amerigo-vespucci).

Knight, Kevin. "Amerigo Vespucci." New Advent, 2012 (http://www.newadvent.org/cathen/15384b.htm).

Knight, Kevin. "Martín Alonso Pinzón." New Advent, 2012 (http://www.newadvent.org/cathen/12104a.htm).

Lyden, Jackie. "New Book Sheds Light on Explorer Vespucci." National Public Radio, July 17, 2011 (http://www.npr.org/templates/story/story.php?storyId=14266532).

Mariner's Museum. "Amerigo Vespucci." 2015 (http://exploration.marinersmuseum.org/subject/amerigo-vespucci/).

NNDB. "Amerigo Vespucci." 2014 (http://www.nndb.com/people/438/000085183/).

Szalay, Jessie. "Amerigo Vespucci: Facts, Biography & Naming of America." Live Science, January 10, 2014 (http://www.livescience.com/42510-amerigo-vespucci.html).

Totally History. "Amerigo Vespucci." 2012 (http://totallyhistory.com/amerigo-vespucci/).

About the Author

Heather Moore Niver writes and edits all types of books for kids of every age. She has also written biographies about Sojourner Truth, Ruth Bader Ginsberg, and Veronica Roth. Niver lives, writes, and edits in New York State.

Photo Credits

Designer: Nicole Russo; Editor: Meredith Day; Photo Researcher: Sherri Jackson